Elfie Shiosaki is a Noongar and Yawuru writer, as well as an Associate Professor at the College of Arts and Social Sciences, Australian National University. Her research and teaching explore Indigenous desires for human rights and self-determination. She was *Westerly* magazine's inaugural Editor for Indigenous Writing (2017–21), and her debut poetry collection *Homecoming* (Magabala Books, 2021) was winner of the Western Australian Premier's Prize for an Emerging Writer, as well as being shortlisted for the Stella Prize and the Prime Minister's Literary Awards, among other prizes.

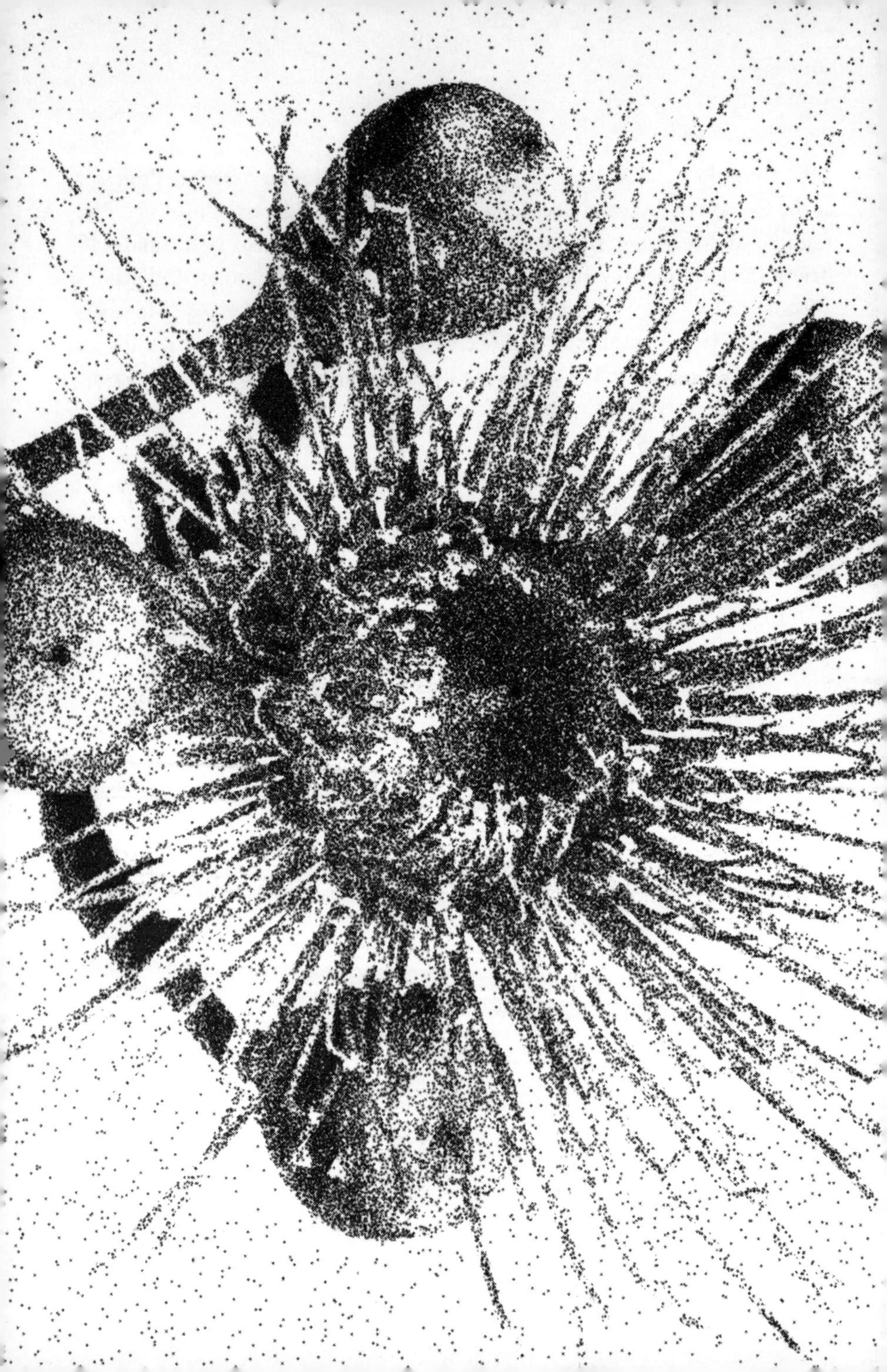

REFUGIA

ELFIE SHIOSAKI

This is a Magabala Book

LEADING PUBLISHER OF ABORIGINAL AND TORRES STRAIT ISLANDER STORYTELLERS.

CHANGING THE WORLD, ONE STORY AT A TIME.

First published 2024
Magabala Books Aboriginal Corporation
1 Bagot Street, Broome, Western Australia
Website: www.magabala.com
Email: sales@magabala.com

Magabala Books is assisted by the Commonwealth Government through Creative Australia, its arts advisory body. The State of Western Australia has made an investment in this project through the Department of Local Government, Sport and Cultural Industries.

Magabala Books is Australia's only independent Aboriginal and Torres Strait Islander publishing house. Magabala Books acknowledges the Traditional Owners of the Country on which we live and work. We recognise the unbroken connection to traditional lands, waters and cultures. Through what we publish, we honour all our Elders, peoples and stories, past, present and future.

Cover Design by Jo Hunt
Cover image Shutterstock
Illustrations by Gene Eaton, Magabala Books
Typeset by Post Pre-press Group
Printed and bound by Griffin Press, South Australia

ISBN (Print) 978-1-922777-13-3
ISBN (ePUB) 978-1-922777-46-1
ISBN (ePDF) 978-1-922777-47-8

A catalogue record for this book is available from the National Library of Australia

This text includes the reproduction of archival material. Readers are advised that this material contains historical terminology when referring to Aboriginal and Torres Strait Islander people.

BEND

A Galaxy of Stories

in cosmic cliffs
womb of dust and gas
a story is born

a stellar nursery
is a blazing birthplace
for remembering, for forgetting

a galactic collision
of time and place
in a glittering skyscape

carved from clouds of cosmic ash
by rays of light
and stellar winds

if a story is a star,
then history is a galaxy
of hundreds of billions of stars

warping space

stretching light from the early universe

        hurtling towards my eyes

Chicxulub Impact / 1829

fateful collision
sea in sky
crashing back down again
demise and burial under burning debris

truth is a story held in ancient sediment in the seabed
but now there is an aperture in the sedimentary records
a muddle of remembering and forgetting
buried under a crushing mass of mud and rock

my hands contain the crash of a star
the collision of sea and sky
the weight of human history
bursting out of itself

a story is where we begin

Mattalan

born from the millennia-old womb of Wilman boodja
with the fresh waters of the Williams River coursing in her veins
she sways like a wattie seedling in the southerly when she learns to walk on the riverbank
her small footprints bury her grandmother's own deeper into the sand
thousands of generations
imprinted into sediment

I return to Williams River two centuries after her birth
my boots sink into the riverbed and my socks fill with sand
I search her night sky
there is only darkness

only a cold sadness seeping into my bones

grandmother, your stars have fallen from the sky in fire and dust
and been cast into the sea

Kingdoms

in black letter shapes on white paper
Daisy Bates inscribes beel-gar,
the people of the Swan River,
in *The Passing of the Aborigines*,[1]
a vibration in the air
never intended to be transcribed into the Roman alphabet

in the reading room of the library / I scream into the spine of the book
Daisy Bates, you even take my name from me / Quiet Please!

kingdoms rise and fall
on the tip of a tongue

take my name
from your tongue

now, it is my turn to speak

Huggins, W.J. 1827, *Captain Stirling's exploring party 50 miles up the Swan River.* National Library of Australia (134156746).

My Fathers

colonial weeds in the soil of memory
proclaim that the founding father of Western Australia is Captain James Stirling
planting feet and flag on ancestral lands of the Whadjuk Noongar
without fatherly love in the vessels of his heart
and making an offering of pistols and swords
swathed in the Union Jack to gods of greed

yet, retrograde amnesia blooms in the mind
corroding and pitting truths into flaky and brittle knowledge

I am not the daughter of Captain Stirling
my fathers are the Whadjuk
born from a Country where the river carves a path from mountain to sea
where the sun rises over the Darling Ranges and falls into the Indian Ocean

we are in the mournful birdsong of the black cockatoo
        flocking before rain

we are in the full moon
                dragging sea onto land and scattering seaweed and blue bottles

we are in the first flint of light
        crowning mountains with golden eastward sky

we are in gusts of the southerly
                carrying smoke haze from bushfires north

a millennia-old Nation overlaid by another
stories buried yet breathing
land and sky meet as feet stamp soil into clouds of dust
dance on Noongar boodja,
        to unearth her memories

Venerate (Good, Not Evil)

Captain James Stirling,
venerated in corroding bronze
under a young London plane tree on Hay Street
unveiled by a future king in 1979
during a heatwave of bunuru season
when white blossoms of jarrah trees swirl
in gusts of the easterly

Captain James Stirling,
by the colony's own boastful handwriting
you are held to account
a decisive encounter gloriously etched into archival memory[2]
    against Bindjareb men, women and children sleeping in their campgrounds

Captain James Stirling,
remain standing with the stars as your cosmic witness
and the truth laid bare
at your feet
    naked in your illegitimacy

future generations
will wonder at the absurdity
of a city that venerates criminals
who did not build a nation
    but savagely tore one down

CAPTAIN JAMES STIRLING
FOUNDER GOVERNOR OF WESTERN AUSTRALIA
1829–1838

ON 28 OCTOBER 1834, CAPTAIN STIRLING LED THE
PINJARRA MASSACRE, ATTACKING BINDJAREB
NOONGAR MEN, WOMEN AND CHILDREN SLEEPING
IN THEIR CAMPGROUNDS AT DAWN

UNVEILED BY
HIS ROYAL HIGHNESS THE PRINCE OF WALES K.G., K.T., G.C.B., P.C.
ON MARCH 10TH, 1979
CELEBRATING THE STATE'S 150TH ANNIVERSARY

DONATED TO THE CITY AND PEOPLE OF PERTH
BY CHANNEL NINE AND RADIO 6KY

it is not too late to turn back, it is never too late

Listen

an oceanic journey on HMS *Success*
to Noongar boodja in 1827
navigating stars
rising and setting in constellation
between Sydney / Hobart / King George Sound / Cape Leeuwin / Rottnest Island

Captain James Stirling, listen
in between the beating breeze and occasional squalls[3]
when you pass through the gust front of the thunderstorm

and the wind drops

and the tide slackens

and the surface of the water reflects the curvature of Earth

and the moon is half crescent

and the starlight bathes you

and your skin soaks in its eternal luminosity

and the stars dip

and float in the water

and you see them below, not above

could you not hear the stars,
singing out to you?

teaching you
to build your campfire
on the shores of the Indian Ocean
and in fire and smoke anticipate the Whadjuk

to welcome you
to ensure your safe passage
to exchange knowledge and stories
to be curious and friendly

to be cared for by Noongar boodja
    until you returned home to your own country
        with your belly full
            and peace in your heart

it never had to be this way

Altered

come with me!
on a tin can rocket ship
jet propelled with escape velocity into an altered universe
            ESCAPE!

daydream with me!
at the edge of our universe
90 billion light years away

    there is a time and place called What Could Have Been

where the sovereignty of the Noongar Nation is unvanquished
the fresh water of the beeliar is unpolluted
and our children sleep
    with deep breaths of uninterrupted peace
                PEACE!

and there are rainbows, kittens and lollipops floating without gravity in space
            KITTENS!

it is nice here!

it did not have to be this way

Captain James Stirling, you did not have to reach for your pistol or sword
you could have reached for the compassion in your heart
the desire to tread lightly on Noongar boodja, without
trampling the spider orchid flat

our children need to know

that it never had to be this way

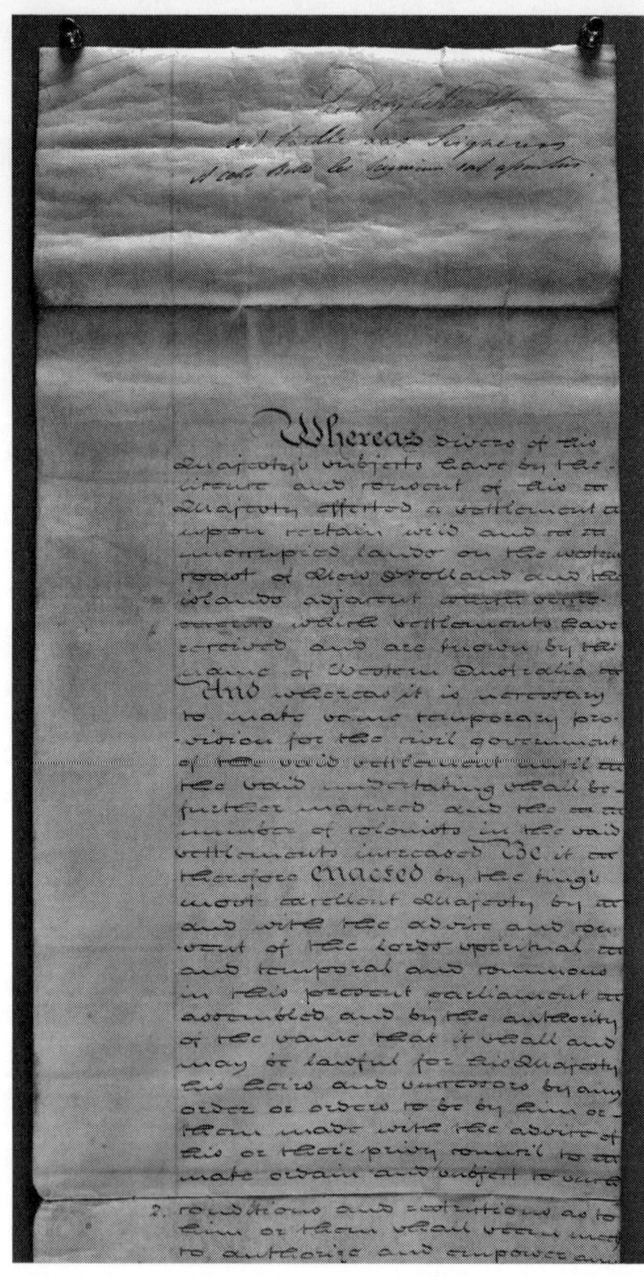
Whereas divers of His Majesty's subjects have by the licence and consent of His Majesty effected a settlement upon certain wild and unoccupied lands on the western coast of New Holland and the islands adjacent thereunto which settlements have received and are known by the name of Western Australia And whereas it is necessary to make some temporary provision for the civil government of the said settlements until the said undertaking shall be further matured and the number of colonists in the said settlements increased Be it therefore enacted by the King's most excellent Majesty by and with the advice and consent of the lords spiritual and temporal and commons in this present parliament assembled and by the authority of the same that it shall and may be lawful for His Majesty his heirs and successors by any order or orders to be by him or them made with the advice of his or their privy council to make ordain and subject to such

2\. conditions and restrictions as to him or them shall seem meet to authorize and empower any

Western Australian Act 1829 (UK). UK Parliamentary Archives (HL/PO/PU/1/1829/10G4n63).

Whereas divers of His Majesty's subjects have by the license and consent of His Majesty effected a settlement upon certain

wild and unoccupied lands

on the western coast of New Holland and the islands adjacent which settlements have received and are

known by the name of Western Australia.[4]

Wild and Unoccupied Lands on the Western Coast of New Holland

on Noongar boodja,
Western Australia writes itself into existence

 a hurried Act
 to forestall a French colony

a lie purported to be law

a piece of paper purported to be nationhood

a story now purported to be history

naming and claiming lands known as intimately to the Whadjuk as the smiling lines around our own grandmothers' eyes

Midnights

neither wild

        nor unoccupied

tell me,

on what lawful grounds did the Empire take possession of Noongar boodja?

False Claims

even now
the Swan River Colony continues
to make false claims
over sovereign bodies

can you not see the light of our youngest stars in Unit 18

fading

in the darkness

of solitary confinement?

come rain, flood and wind, I fear we have built our house on shaky foundations

On the Edge

in a confluence
two currents meet
on the edge
of the beeliar

the Whadjuk
and Captain James Stirling
those born under the Milky Way
and those born under St George's cross, a red rose and the Three Lions

currents that do not converge
but collide
the cold northward-flowing current
breathing fog over the beeliar in
                    wave crests carrying
                    dolphins herding
                    schools of fish
                    splashing in the shallows

mimicking 'how do you do?' and cheering the bugle[5]
young Whadjuk men cast down their spears and kangaroo skin cloaks in
  diplomacy
friendship and curiosity
on the edge

a boundary that will be raked over by boots
by a false declaration of sovereignty
and proclamation of settlement of wild and unoccupied lands[6]
a sacred boundary separating friendship from war, curiosity from oppression

stemming a king tide of violence

Shores

on the shores of the beeliar
heels burying deeper into cool river sand
where bulrushes weave nesting grounds for the black swan into
  the river
    peace is built in marriage ceremonies between Noongar, mixing blood,
    soil and bone

on the shores of the Indian Ocean
palms clapping ochre into chalky dust
where crayfish shell glints from shallow pools in the fringe reef
    peace is built on the shared boundaries of Noongar and Yamatji

yet, on the shores of the North Sea
fingertips gripping axe haft
where shipyards scuttle oak forests into keels and frames
    ships are built to carry guns and cannons

may the ambition of our hearts

be peace,

    not expansion

be family,

    not empire

be contentment,

    not a lusty thirst for sweet waters that do not belong to us

Treasure Troves

one man's Captain
another's pirate
plundering Noongar boodja
trunk and branches cut down
sold off to a ship builder
and carved into an ornate gunport in the Captain's great cabin
uncommon wealth
hoarded in the Empire's treasure troves

Impact Event

Temple station is thick with bodies at 8am. On the platform, I plant the Aboriginal flag and brace for impact, as though it is a blazing comet with a black, yellow and red tail streaking across the northern hemisphere.

Except there is no impact, no rupture of the earth. In fact, no passengers acknowledge the existence of the flag, side-stepping it in a hurry to board the train. The flag gently flutters in the piston wind.

four stripes of white curtains
horizontal, diagonal and vertical
on a blue cyclorama
with a red cross suspended over the stage
are only cuts of cloth
forsaken on Noongar boodja

swarmed by flying ants in djeran season

tattered by the gusting southerly in kambarang

faded in the relentless heatwave of bunuru

I board the next train for Kew Gardens to continue my research in The National Archives. Sovereign voices speaking from within the Empire burn my ears until all I can hear is heat and light and my heart blazes.

if it was not the flag
then it was the violence

that was the Swan River Colony's principal means of expansion[7]

ENCOUNTER WITH THE NATIVES
IN THE PINJARRA DISTRICT,
ON THE BANKS OF THE MURRAY.

THE report of this successful and decisive encounter with the Natives of the Murray, who have for some time been the terror of the neighbourhood, was received with general satisfaction,—an opinion having prevailed that the system of lenity and forbearance hitherto adopted by the Government was not calculated to ensure safety to either the lives or property of the settlers. We have not space to revert to the many atrocities committed by the tribe, upon which at length retribution has fallen; they are, however, within the recollection of our Readers, having but recently transpired, and will fully justify the severity of the punishment.—A Gentleman, an eye witness, has obligingly favored us with the following narrative of the encounter; from the respectability of the party, the accuracy of this report may be implicitly relied upon.

1834, 'Encounter with the Natives in the Pinjarra District, on the Banks of the Murray,' *The Perth Gazette*, 1 November, p. 382. State Library of Western Australia.

The Accuracy of This Report may be Implicitly Relied Upon

~~decisive encounter~~ massacre

~~terror of the neighbourhood~~ traditional owners

received with general satisfaction

~~system of lenience and forbearance~~ systemic violence

~~settlers~~ ?

~~atrocities committed by the tribe~~ self-defence

~~punishment~~ crime

~~Gentleman~~ Criminal

~~respectability~~ criminality

do not speak to me of accuracy

do not speak to me of implicitness

your words melt on my palm like the brittle hail stones of makuru season

After a consultation over the prisoners, it was resolved to set them free, for the purpose of fully explaining to the remnant of the tribe the cause of the chastisement which had been inflicted, and to bear a message to the effect that

"if they again offered to spear white men or their cattle, or to revenge in any way the punishment which had just been inflicted on them for their numerous murders and outrages, four times the present number of men would proceed amongst them and

destroy every man,

woman

and child."[8]

The Fujiwhara Effect

She waded out onto the shallow sandbank at City Beach, her calves trawling though the northerly current. Digging her toes into the sand, she closed her eyes and gave her memories of the archive to the sea. The current swiftly carried them out into the indigo waters of the Indian Ocean.

The sea relieved her mind with the ebb and flow of its salty tides for only a season.

In the spring, when the southerly chopped at the Indian Ocean, the dumpers at City Beach crashed her memories onto the sandbank and they floated on the surface of the water in white soapy foam.

In the summer, when the full moon dragged the Indian Ocean onto the land, the tide heaved her memories up onto the sand, dragging them through shells and cuttlefish bones to the wrack line.

In the autumn, when Tropical Cyclone Seroja formed off the West Australian coast, wind gusts and heavy rain littered the shoreline with an ocean of debris and memories.

She screamed at the sea for refusing to hold her pain in its watery hands and give her relief.

Black Hole

I

swirling
within a glowing disc
birthed by a dying star

    twinkling
    from four million suns
    within the caustic heart of the Milky Way

bending and stretching
time and space around itself
even light cannot escape

its gravitational field
tenderly embracing stars and dust
only for the black hole to eat them alive

we cross the event horizon, the boundary between light and darkness
into a loop in time
we begin in the future
    end in the past
        and go back to the future again

now we are stuck in a time loop
and we cannot remember if it is 1834
or 2020 when we march on Riverside Drive

    we can only remember grief

now we are stuck in a time loop
tangled in a sticky web of cause and effect
and they warned us

once you cross the event horizon
you can never go back
not even the light

we can never go back
to a time of not knowing

II

this ride on the Gravitron
is going way too fast
laughter turns into shrieking

I would like to get off!

I would like it to stop!

1834 / 2020 / 1834 / 2020 / 1834

but the centrifugal force pins me against the wall
and my feet cannot touch the ground
and it is swirling

and swirling

and swirling

III

my hope for us
is that we know
when to hop off the ride

to forgive the past

before we break
into uncountable pieces
of swirling grief

BREAK

All the Things

She drives the car on all the highways to the creek.

She eats all the biscuits on the first morning.

She drinks all the coffee and smokes all the cigarettes, sometimes on her own, sometimes with strangers on the bank of the creek.

She hates all the words she writes on the pages.

She tears out all the pages.

She wonders if she will ever be loved again.

She sleeps in the deck chair on the verandah, sometimes in the morning, sometimes in the afternoon.

She wears a black felt hat with a woven band, just to feel something.

She wonders if Jay Swan will ever turn up at her door on police business.

She wades out into the creek in her Adidas shorts and floats on her back, until the sun lights up her thighs under the water.

She writes a list of all the things that broke her heart that year.

Just that year. 2020.

She goes on the boat and sees the humpback whale crest and lunge out of the Southern Ocean with all the joy.

It does not seem to have any body image issues.

She gets stung by the bull ant sitting on the bank of the creek.

She adds that to the list:

> the bushfires,
>
> the pandemic,
>
> the police brutality,
>
> and her fear that the stars have fallen from the sky and set the world on fire.

When she has done all the things, she wonders if she is feeling better.

Then she drives the car on all the highways home.

Supernova

Spluttering, she collapses into herself in explosive spitting and choking.

Overheating, her swollen outer layers engorge, transforming her into a Red Giant.

She is unstable, sometimes burning furiously, other times cooling down.

Pulsating, she throws off her outer layers and enshrouds herself in a cocoon of gas and dust.

She blows herself apart in a luminous stellar explosion, outshining all of the other stars for a week or so.

Then she fades,

scattering elements and debris into space,

and sprinkling Earth

with interstellar dust grains.

No longer a star in her grandmothers' sky.

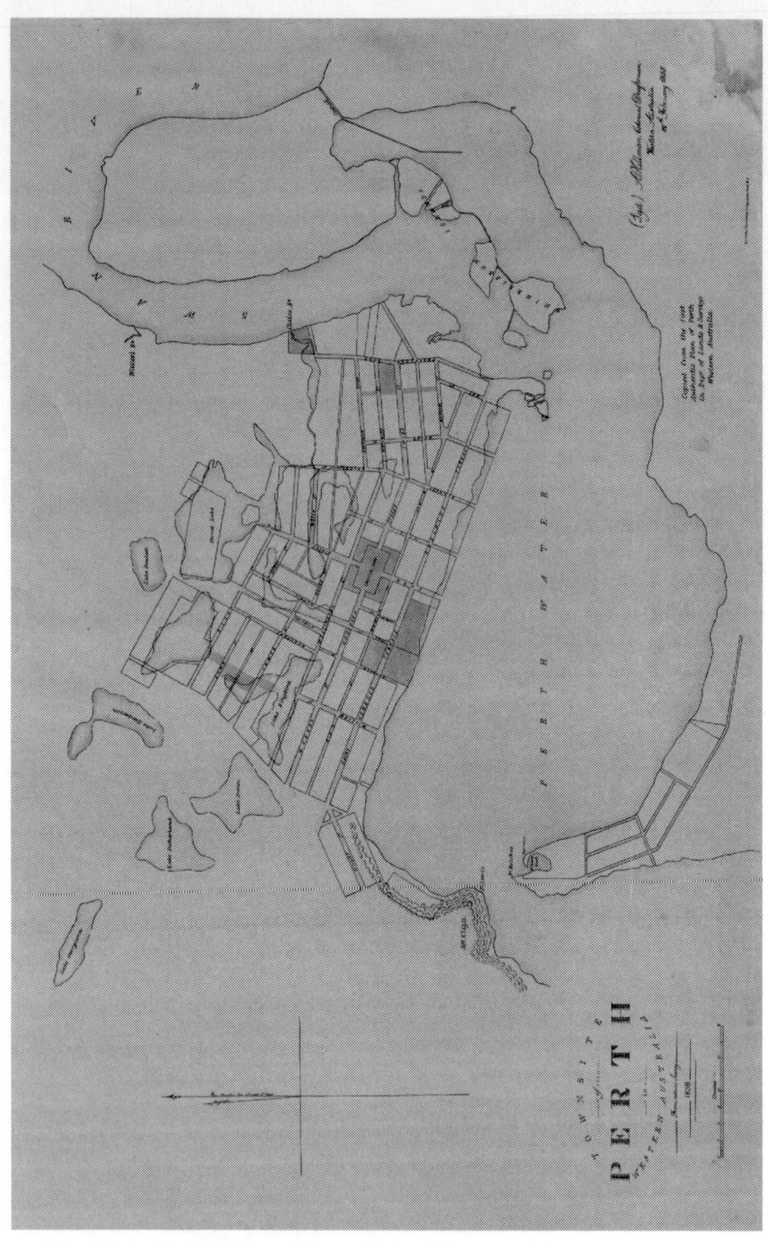

Hillman, A. 1838, 'Plan of townsite of Perth, Western Australia.'
State Library of Western Australia (B/1/32).

Dust and Bones

buried
under steel and reinforced concrete

overlaid
by colonial imaginations of development

submerged
into the water table beneath the city

remnants of interconnected freshwater wetlands, swamps and lakes
waterways that seasonally flooded and cleansed Whadjuk boodja
sheltered water birds, frogs, gilgies and turtles
and carried songlines in her swollen belly

drained and filled
in arrogant miscalculation
the Empire's first act of ecological colonisation on Noongar boodja
orchestrating the ebb and flow of the beeliar to the song of 'Rule, Britannia!'

> Rule, Britannia! Britannia, rule the waves!
> Britons never, never, never will be slaves.

Swan River Colony, you take without ever giving in return
even the fresh waters from your children's veins
        and the oxygen from their lungs

you take until all that is left
is the dust from their bones

Burial Grounds

I stand on burial grounds
of interconnected wetlands
overlaid
vanished
          vanquished?

blood drained in a pale-skinned landscape
gatekept by stony Roe and Forrest

                                        I stand on your burial grounds
                                        centuries of debris crush your chest
                                                                      slow your heart beat

                                        I want you to heave and gasp
                                        Come alive!

I stand on burial grounds
listening for buried beating
yet only hear
vibrations of a city constructed of steel and concrete

willie wagtail resting on electric wire
its birdsong muffled
by construction sites
in wistful incantation to gods of greed

if you rumble deep from under the bitumen, will I hear you then?
    will the water table draw up and flood the city?

I stand on your burial grounds
    wasted tears fall on dusty concrete
        where wetlands used to flow

Wicked Seeds

Swan River Colony,
your establishment the violent genesis
of shifting temperature and weather patterns
the beginning of the end
planting wicked seeds
of greed and corruption
an invasive species
threatening Noongar boodja

Nixon, C.M. 1894, 'Fremantle Harbour, blasting.' State Library of Western Australia (BA1328/10).

Fremantle Harbour

the memory of CY O'Connor's tragedy ebbs and flows
where river meets sea meets sunset
the construction of Fremantle Harbour
for royal mail contractors shipping news from London to Noongar boodja

his plans demolish the rocky limestone bar with explosives
dredge the sand shoals
erode the sacred boundary between fresh and salt waters
an estuary intermediatory

in violent folly, flooding the beeliar with Indian Ocean
you claim to be master
but you are slave
to gold and glory

in 1897 RMS *Himalaya* berthed in South Quay
with mail from London
primitive science stowed in its cabin
        dashing Noongar boodja on the rocks of ecological catastrophe

                a Country cultivated by thousands of generations of hands

in your arrogance
you claim what you have created is good
and the harbour becomes a golden idol
with offerings of fresh water from your own children's lips

Bicentennial Never

200 years
is time the stars
do not count

200 years
is time vanishing
in their twinkle

Swan River Colony,
when you have cared for the beeliar
when you have safeguarded its fresh waters from pollution
when you have protected the nesting grounds of its water birds
when you have given our children clean water to drink

for millennia
for uncountable time
for the lifetime of a star

then I will gather
on the banks of the beeliar
as the full moon rises over the hills
to celebrate,
to count the time

Wadjemup

Wadjemup
the oldest prison in Western Australia
paradise rebuilt as misery in 1838

more than 3700 Aboriginal men and boys
some as young as eight years old
prisoners of war in the Swan River Colony

their starlight blacked out
by disease, murder and execution
many becoming the first deaths in custody in the state

the Rottnest Island Authority did not speak of the island
as the largest site of deaths in custody in Australia
instead, tourists danced on graves
            and left beer cans there

an island
is a prison
is a playground
is a holiday
from the heaviness of truth

an island
is a prison
is a playground
is a holiday
from the stamina of holding ourselves

the way land holds history

and treads blood memory

and remembers

the story told in the soil of Wadjemup

once again, we light our campfires
at South Beach
to signal our love in fire and smoke

our lamenting remembrance
for the men and boys taken
for those who remain

Monsters

Wadjemup prison
an embryo
for a monster
reborn as
Banksia Hill Detention Centre

we have been here before

THE NATIVES.

The Natives, principally women, have been in and about Perth for the past fortnight, but not in any considerable numbers. Their object in visiting us, they say is, to renew the fri-ndly understanding which existed previously to the affair at Fremantle, and which was followed up by bloodshed and murder. If they are permitted to enter the town, they ought, we are of opinion, never to be allowed to be out of the sight of some authorized persons, who should have the power of controlling the conduct of individuals towards them, at the same time, that they protect the public from any aggression on the part of the natives. We must say

1833, 'The Natives,' *The Perth Gazette*, 10 August, p. 126.

Misunderstanding

Swan River Colony,
what were the terms of our understanding?

friendly understandings
between the Whadjuk and the colony
were washed away
in the high tide
that carried the HMS *Challenger*
to the mouth of the beeliar in 1829
a warship carrying cannons and guns
when Captain Charles Fremantle took possession of New Holland
and hoisted the British flag at the river mouth
only to fell, limb and buck our grandmother tree
her crown cast into dust

our understanding was steeped in marauding acts of war, not friendship
our understanding was never friendly

In and About Perth

sweltering as we march along Riverside Drive
blue sky spinning
black road tilting

overheated politics on a 40-degree day

blue shirts lining the street blur into the fresh waters of the beeliar
        never to be allowed to be out of the sight of some authorised person

                with Glock 22 .40-calibre pistols
        they protect the public from any aggression on the part of the native

we have been here before
        to renew the friendly understanding

it was only the sherbet fizz in a jug of Pimms
talking and laughing cheeks flushed with my sisters
in the courtyard of Picabar

that carried my weary spirit home on Invasion Day

Paper Cuts

between the indexed pages
of a dictionary of international law
a war of words wages

opening the time-worn cover of *Dictionnaire de droit international public et privé*, booming muskets sound with bass

as the largest empire the world has ever seen reaches its territorial peak
amassing almost one quarter of Earth's surface area
and more than 90 per cent of Moon's,
its lust for celestial bodies only restrained by Earth's own
atmospheric skin

in the silence of contemplation, distinguished Argentinian jurist Carlos Calvo
takes his pen
and defines
'invasion'

ENVAHISSEMENT. Occupation by force of the territory of others. (See INVASION, OCCUPATION.)

INVASION. Irruption by an army or a large multitude of people into another land in order to seize it: this is how one could describe the invasion of the Roman Empire by the Barbarians. In a more modern sense, it is the action of invading a country by force of arms, of penetrating it militarily. (See ENVAHISSEMENT, OCCUPATION.)

even then
it was defined as an invasion,
an occupation by force of the territory of the Noongar Nation

an irruption by an army
    in order to seize it
an action of invading a country by force of arms

> All continental war begins with an invasion; because one of the belligerents invades the territory of the other (See WAR, BELLIGERANT); and invasion, if it is not repulsed and if it continues, results in occupation or conquest. (See those words.)[9]

a belligerent invading the territory of the Noongar Nation
with force
without negotiation
and resisted by its people

yet, my hand shakes
when I take my pen
and write
    'Noongar boodja was invaded by the British military in 1829.'

fearing death
by a thousand paper cuts from the literary canon

Grandfather

a scrap of knowledge
preserved in a century-old notebook of mirrored mazes
a snippet of conversation
between my grandmother's grandfather, Edward Harris,
and self-proclaimed anthropologist Daisy Bates
on the banks of the beeliar in Guildford

There has never been an attempt to annex neighbouring tribal territory,

        Grandfather teaches us.

The boundaries of each tribe are as well known to the members as their own home waters.

Of course there have been intertribal quarrels,

But these do not result in the acquisition of fresh territory,

no matter which tribe is victorious.

        His shrines are in his own country

and he thinks perhaps

that the other man's shrines

would be 'no good' to him.[10]

not lost in Daisy Bates' clumsy translation
an understanding that Noongar law
could never be transplanted
from one Country to take possession of another

its roots run too deep

Armour

remnant news
in *The Perth Gazette*
of an attempt to negotiate a peace treaty
by Noongar grandmothers in 1833

a trace
of their recognition
by the Swan River Colony

a trace
of negotiation nation to nation
between the Noongar Nation and the colony

a trace
of their desire for a settlement
to end bloodshed and murder

a faint trace

is a crack

in the valiant armour

of *terra nullius*

worn by the colonial archive

Refusal

I am
a star

in the constellation of blak resistance
refusing to shine with resilience
for a time

I am
a star

I shine
I am dull

I orbit the galaxy
I am cast into the sea

I am cosmic fire
I am base and brittle

I am in the constellation

whether I resist

whether I am resilient

whether you can see me or not

Sing

I

defeat strikes
like bolts of lightning
hitting the 200-year-old jarrah tree in the Perth Hills

coursing with current
heating
steaming

boiling water in its tree roots
bursting into flames from within its trunk
exploding strips of eucalypt bark from its branches

bending
then bouncing back
shuddering from the collision between earth and sky

the tree is older than the Swan River Colony
after centuries of thunderstorms sparking the bushfires of bunuru
it remains standing

        and its burnt-out tree hollows have become nests for the black cockatoo

even in defeat
it is yet to surrender

II

in swirling embers and smoke
feet stamping on ash
I sing for

buds

          and shoots

I sing for regeneration

BUD

From Ashes

from ashes
littered on Noongar boodja
remnant cries for justice
swirling in the southerly
from carbon formed within stars
from stardust

we build a nation

we coalesce in stars

we constellate[11]

Non-Union

I refuse
to walk on Country
wounded
        limping
like a broken femur that will not heal
swelling
        tenderness
                aching pain
without stability
or blood supply to bone

you see, I want to take great strides through Boranup Forest where ancient karri trees intone history

I want to leap over fallen branches
        climb over trunks
                and blaze a new trail through the forest

in Lake Cave, where rainfall travels through limestone into a deep chamber
and a starry night is suspended in stromatolites
twinkling in pools of water
I bathe in eternal luminescence
and soak grief out of my bones

I leap

and I stride

I climb

I leap

I stride

I climb

Cleansing

the colony has polluted the beeliar
now its brackish waters pump in our veins
our blood cries out
for rain

for cleansing

for forgiveness

send the rain!
to soak me to the bone

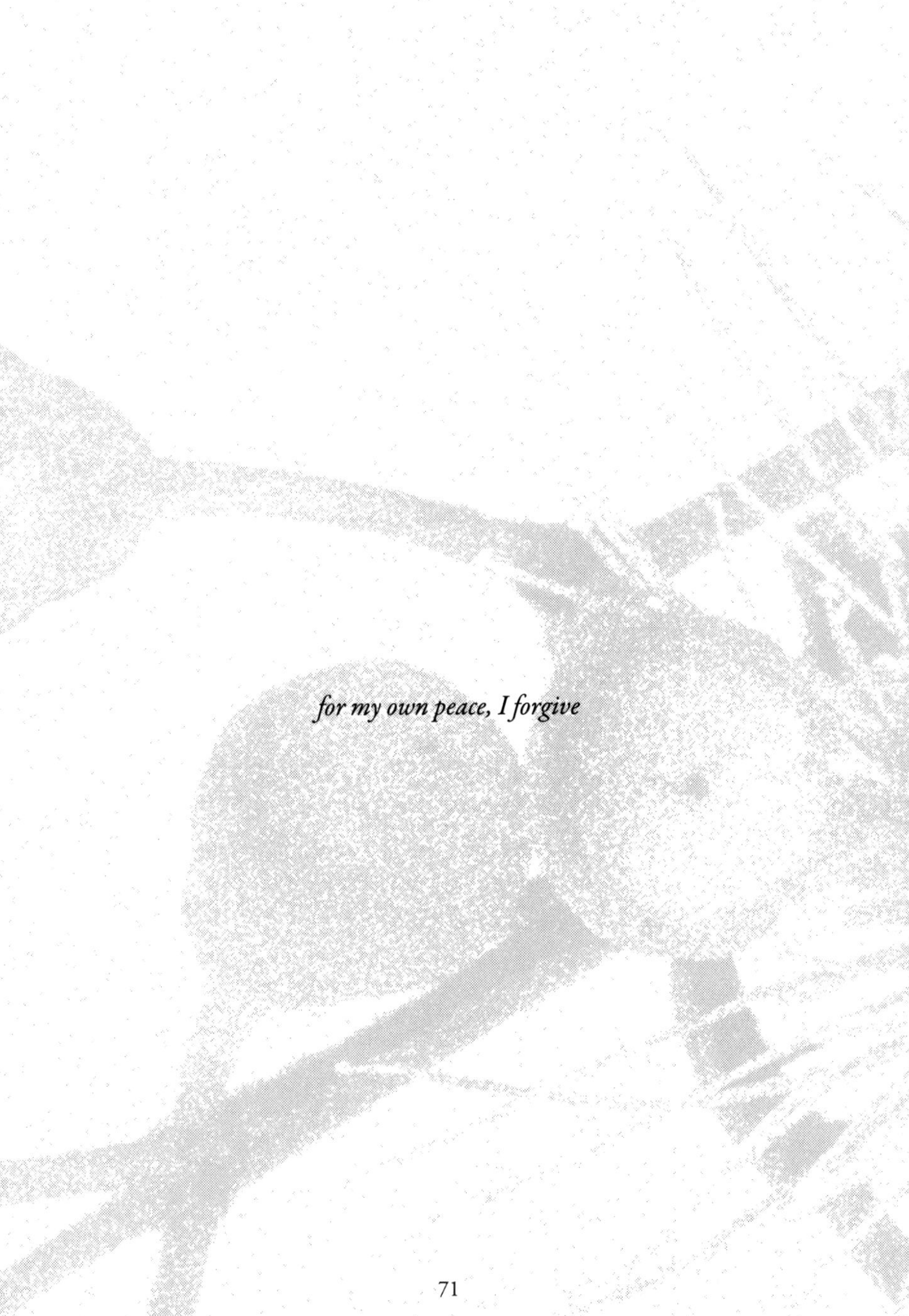

for my own peace, I forgive

Revival

I no longer see
the ghosts of my past
in my future

Sirius

I was born
from the womb of the beeliar
with a temperament for change
and an unwillingness
to
            let
                        be
with its fresh waters in my veins
none can divert my course

my heart knows
in a thousand generations
my river
will carve a starward path from
my mountain to
my sea to
my sky

in its untamed ebb and flow
my river returns to water ice held in the asteroid belt
pulls downwards
the brightest star in the galaxy
            a new sun
                        a new dawn
                                    a new day on Noongar boodja

Home Sick

before we part, my love

I weave strands of my hair

into the branches of the paperbark

rooted in river sand

its branches bend leaves into the beeliar

into the ebb and flow

where the clouds fall from the sky

into the shallow silty waters of the riverbank

our secret place

where the easterly whispers words into the rustling leaves of the paperbark

where the fresh water currents ebb sentences to the shore

where the pelicans carry stories from salt to fresh waters in their beaks

where you unwrap my grief from my skin

a lock of hair

to remind you of me

call me home

before you forget me

Whadjuk Boodja

now
with a border between us

you are
the unanswered call to my birdsong

Refugia

I

The first ever recorded sighting of the sapling was in the summer of 2029. Rising early to water her lawn on Glendower Street, a young woman in North Perth had photographed its stem and infant eucalypt leaf unearthing in the dawn light. The street was rowed with 1930s red-brick cottages and climbing roses wilting onto peeling white picket fences.

That day the city was blanketed in a dusty heat carried over the Darling Ranges by the easterly.

No relief.

At that time, no one knew that the eucalypt had sprung from ancient root systems buried deep within the wetlands of Hyde Park across the street. When the balance of the world had upended two centuries ago, the roots hibernated under the earth, cooling and slowing their breath.

Their enduring inability to define this plant life unsettled academics at the School of Biological Sciences. They had found lonely solace in dominating the natural world and collecting and classifying its most sacred inner thoughts. The director of Kings Park and Botanic Garden named and claimed the life as

eucalyptus avia.

When the tree in her front garden became overgrown with silver leaves and red flowers, its trunk and branches reaching for the chimney crown on the tin roof, the young woman cut it down

with a chainsaw,

fearing that its root system would destabilise the foundation of her newly purchased property.

Yet the sapling re-sprouted, and many others began to unearth themselves around North Perth. *Avia* had tilted the balance of the suburb, its tendrils rocking residents back and forth in an uneasy embrace.

The cutting down, digging up and burning of the trees only enlivened their growth until the suburb became a thick forest of silver leaves. Their root systems cracked open the footpaths, roads and foundations of every house and building, bending and breaking them to

the will of a new master.

By the end of summer, North Perth had become

a rubble of concrete, steel and dust.

Displaced from their homes, residents sought refuge in other areas of the city. Internally Displaced Persons camps were erected on the fringe of the Kalamunda hills to provide emergency accommodation to families who had nowhere else to go,

no one to turn to.

The Premier declared a state of emergency and the city became overrun with scientists from around the world wearing hazmat suits attempting to contain the spread of *avia* in soil from their equipment and shoes. All were perplexed by its origins and unable to

stem its woody tide.

II

At that time, no one knew that pollen from the red blossoms unfurling on *avia* was being carried in the dusty easterly.

It clung to their lungs

and was pollinated in polite conversation between neighbours.

The outbreak spread and soon residents were confined to their homes for weeks, unable to travel freely around the city for fear of treading soil from one suburb to another. But the hedonism in their hearts overpowered them, and police were often called to break up gatherings in homes, backyards, laneways and Scarborough Beach.

By the end of autumn, Perth city had become overrun by blossoming red flowers.

III

All residents on the Swan Coastal Plain had now been displaced, and the beeliar snaked its way to the Indian Ocean

unencumbered.

Hundreds lined the South Perth foreshore to witness the crumbling of the Rio Tinto building as it bent and broke under a towering forest that crushed its torso and lungs. The building expired in a red dust cloud; its last heaving breath hung over the city for days, like thick pollution. In the crushing, residents were struck by the

impermanence

of steel and reinforced concrete frameworks, and curtain walls of polished stone.

The city was entombed in a twisted wreath of trunks and branches, which sparkled with silver glitter when the sun rose over the Darling Ranges each winter morning. Car honks, screeching brakes of Transperth buses and early Sunday morning drum and bass fell silent.

The city began to hum

with circadian rhythm.

IV

Fearing the spread of *avia* to other regions of the south west, by spring the Premier declared Perth city a prohibited area. Residents were unable to ever return to their homes, and the tented suburbs around the Kalamunda hills became reified with white goods and satellite dishes.

A new balance on the Swan Coastal Plain had

tipped.

Over the years, Perth city became

a sprawling womb

for new plant and animal life, unordered by columns and rows of cottages and picket fences. The black cockatoo returned to nest in *avia*, filling its branches with birdsong.

The day the fresh waters of the beeliar broke the embankments of Elizabeth Quay, life was returned to the ancient wetlands of the city. The tides once again ebbed and flowed with the full belly of the moon. When the tide was at its highest point, the waters in the wetlands at Hyde Park trickled towards the river and were carried out into the Indian Ocean.

After centuries of dampened displacement, the bodies of fresh and salt waters were tenderly

reunited

in an historic reckoning.

Everlasting

wildflowers
buried in the shallow loam of Mullewa
bloom to blazon the desert with pink stars
they bloom for the ancient seabed
for the rocky outcrops
for the dusty easterly
for the kangaroo, emu and goanna
for the Milky Way
never for the pages of a botanist's journal
or even the human eye

only for the joy of wholly bursting into colour skyward

we attune ourselves
to the truth that all who spring from soil
do not return to earth
we are destined to burn and blaze
destined to return to stars

we are wildflowers carpeting the Mid West

we are pink stars scattered across the galaxy

we are everlasting

The Sapling

young one

you are

a sapling taking root between layers of soil and rock
soaking up the fresh waters of the Swan and Williams Rivers
your eucalypt leaves whispering stories
in winds from many homelands

Broome / Osaka / London / Dublin

you shoot after the bushfires in bunuru season
when dark, stringy bark carried fire up into the leafy crown of your centuries-old grandmother tree
in heat and smoke, seed pods opened
and you fell from her canopy
into ash and soil

in the storms of djilba season
the agile branches of your aunty's tree
bend to shelter you from strong winds and heavy rains
her knotted trunk stands between you and the storm
keeping you rooted in Country

in the heatwaves of birak season
the lustrous canopy of your nana's tree
reflects the sun to protect you from the searing midday heat
her tree crown garlanded with clusters of white flowers
keeping you cared for by Country

young one

one day

your roots will run deep into the heart of Country

    your trunk will preserve climate stories in its growth rings

hollowed out from cleansing bushfires, it will become a nest for black cockatoo and her chicks

    your branches will shelter banksia and grass trees

your logs will become burrows for bandicoot and quoll

    every birak you will burst into white blossoms

you will be our grandfather tree
in our towering jarrah forest
your trunk and branches reaching for stars

Noongar Rising

in ember and ash
the heart of the Noongar Nation
beats buried

radiant heat and light
without combustion
in the violent debris
            of the Swan River Colony

soaring above the nation
riding the thermal updrafts sky-high
the firehawk swoops

descending to seize with conviction
glowing embers
in its talons

spreading wildfires
to set the grass alight
and smoke out its flinching prey

from Kaart Gennunginyup Bo, the place to look afar,
we see the Noongar Nation

rise from ashes

rise above the colony

rise into stars

Author's Note

This collection has been creatively nurtured by NASA's James Webb Space Telescope's first year of science. In the same way the Webb Telescope seeks new understandings of the formation of the first stars and galaxies, this collection seeks new understandings of the formation of the Swan River Colony in Western Australia in 1829. The sovereignty of the Noongar Nation comes into starlight.

Refugia is a tribute to the continuity of Noongar boodja (Country), its six seasons (birak, bunuru, djeran, makuru, djilba and kambarang), its beeliar (rivers), and the refuge it gives to all of us.

I acknowledge Verve Poetry Press for supporting the development of some of the writing in this collection and publishing 'Mattalan', 'My Fathers' and 'Dust and Bones' in *Across Borders: An Anthology of New Poems from the Commonwealth* (2022). I thank the Stella Prize for generously gifting me a two-week writer's residency to support the completion of my manuscript. I also thank the extraordinary archivists at the State Records Office of Western Australia, the State Library of Western Australia, the National Library of Australia and the UK Parliamentary Archives for supporting my archival research.

I thank the team at Magabala Books, in particular my exceptional editor Arlie Alizzi, Rachel Bin Salleh and Xenica Ayling, for continuing to nurture the development of my writing and for holding my stories in safe hands.

Endnotes

1 Bates, Daisy 1944, *The passing of the Aborigines: a lifetime spent among the natives of Australia*, Murray, London.

2 1834, 'Encounter with the Natives in the Pinjarra District, on the Banks of the Murray,' *The Perth Gazette*, 1 November, p. 382.

3 Gilbert, Augustus H. 1906, 'An Account of the Expedition of H.M.S *Success*, Captain James Stirling, RN, from Sydney, to the Swan River, in 1827.'

4 *Western Australian Act* 1829 (UK). UK Parliamentary Archives (HL/PO/PU/1/1829/10G4n63).

5 Green, Neville 1984, *Broken spears: Aborigines and Europeans in the southwest of Australia*, Focus Education Services, Perth, p. 6.

6 *Western Australian Act* 1829 (UK).

7 Wolfe, Patrick 2006, 'Settler Colonialism and the Elimination of the Native,' *Journal of Genocide Research*, 8:4, p. 392.

8 'Encounter with the Natives in the Pinjarra District.'

9 Calvo, Carlos 1885, *Dictionnaire de droit international public et privé*, vol 1, Puttkammer & Muhlbrecht, Berlin, pp. 297, 403. Translated by Dr Rowan Nicholson and cited in Nicholson, R. 2019, 'Was the colonisation of Australia an invasion of sovereign territory?' *Melbourne Journal of International Law*, 20:2, pp. 493–529.

10 'Notes compiled at Guilford,' Papers of Daisy Bates, National Library of Australia, MS 365, 72/53-64, p. 17.

11 This poem responds to East Timorese Prime Minister Xanana Gusmão's reflection in 2005: 'Forgive each other, forget the past, let us build the nation from ashes once again.'